Toddler Discipline

The Ultimate Guide to
Raising Children
With Positive Discipline

By

Marvin B. Gift

with Sandy Pardee

Copyright © 2017

Disclaimer

Table of Content

Introduction

Picked up my computer this particular day and just decided to type in a few strings of words on the Google Search bar about toddlers. I was shocked by the first suggestion and others. I remembered that day I started with why do toddler. .. And as Google would have it, I saw: why do toddlers bite, why do toddlers have tantrums, why do toddlers have big stomachs, why do toddlers hit etc. A toddler having big stomach didn't get a lot of interest from me, but the other three suggestions gave me a reason to write this book. Bite, tantrums and hit all pointed to one fact which we all know is true. Toddlers are real trouble. These sweet beings are still new to the world, they are starting to walk, they still wear diapers and they are still babies with the cute smile and angelic laugh but they can know the difference between right and wrong. The knowledge of right and wrong begins at this stage and it would be very sad if we overlook their flaws and adamancy. Discipline was the first thing which came to mind. But when I thought of the crying faces of those cute pumpkins then I added the word positive to the equation. Positive disciple. Hence the sub-topic: the ultimate guide to raising children with positive discipline. And that's the genesis of this book. Toddler discipline is something we must understand and practice. I can tell you, raising a child is no easy process and if we want to do that, it should be done the right way.

For every reaction, there is an equally opposite reaction. For every demonstration of positive discipline, there is always a response. It could be positive or negative. This book is here to get you into the minds of the toddler, it is here to help you understand them, take the right step, correct them without hurting their fragile feelings, discipline in an extraordinary way and most of all- love them more.

Since we know that child discipline is an effective method to prevent the future behavioral problems in children, we know that we are doing the right thing for these little ones. We are not only doing the right thing for them alone, but for ourselves, the country, the next generation to come and the world. A family is the smallest unit of the society, several of those society forms a community, several communities forms a state and it goes on and on. A child with good discipline standards affects his/her peers, affects the society and even the community.

It is horrendous that nowadays, indiscipline is the other of the day. Young children, teenagers and even youths are becoming almost uncontrollable day by day. So the need to instill discipline in a toddler becomes compulsory. Even the good book says "Train a child in

2

the way he should go, and when he is old he will not turn from it." Proverbs 22:6 (NIV). Read this book carefully and a life of positive discipline as well as a positive response from your child is guaranteed.

Chapter 1

Understanding Toddlers

First, we may not be able to understand what we don't know. So for those who may be new to child care, this is for you - Who is a toddler? The Merriam-Webster Dictionary defines the word toddler as a young child who is just learning to walk; one that toddles; especially a young child. I can't debase the above meaning given to the word toddler by lexicographers, but I can say, that that definition is very shallow because basing your characteristics on an entity based on just one qualification, that is movement in this case could be very myopic. Some children may not be able to learn out to work until they are five, can we say they have not been toddlers before then? No. Then who is a toddler? A toddler is a child between the age brackets of 12 to 36 months. Over the years, the age bracket has become disagreed or not just fixed, but a book by the Santa Cruz Toddler Center in 1993 "1,2,3... The Toddler Years." Give the following views about the varying ages of the toddler.

"It starts somewhere, a child's first birthday and continues until about the age of three . . . Toddlers have the right to be respected for who they are now. Not dependent babies. But also not yet capable preschoolers. Respect means:

- Treating each child as a special individual with important thoughts, feelings and needs.

- Giving children the opportunity to grow and learn at their own pace.

- Allowing children the freedom to create and master their own challenges.

This an age when children are constantly on the move. They learn about the world by exploring it. They want to do everything right now, (often) all by themselves."

Even though the first paragraph had given us what we wanted, some important nuggets of what we would be discussing later in this book were there to give you a hint on what would be coming.

Toddlers are curious, information-seeking individuals. They always want to do more than they can do or more than we let them. Concepts which were not so meaningful some months ago would become fully utilize. Concepts like size, shape and space. They begin to welcome different changes which must have existed for a long time but because they lack the access to it. Concepts like the growing use of imagination. This brings them to the fundamental make believe world where they pretend to be something else or imagining that one object is something else. It also helps them to fantasize properly.

Words become very important to them, even though they are not yet proficient enough to verbally express themselves. They result into imitation accompanied by incoherent verbal explanations.

Movement becomes very important as it opens opportunities by giving them time and space to experience, discover and learn by imitation or doing. Motor development would become an important aspect of their life too. Walking, running, jumping, climbing, throwing, kicking and all other modes of action become something of fun and satisfaction. It's like when a child is in the toddler stage, the world is telling him or her; here I am, know and experience me. And the mental and physical development are made for this. Additionally, music becomes a thing of joy as it allows for movement. Have you ever thought of this 'when I was young, who taught me to dance?' We notice that dance, which is the response of body part in response to music is innate. At this stage of life, the child finds his own personal rhythm. And this supports the child's growing self-concept. That means that it entails what the child thinks about himself when it comes to capabilities, self-worth and physical characteristics. It's no news to us that a child's self-concept has effects on everything he/she does and can be greatly affected by feedback from important people in the child's life. In this manner, toddlers would always want approval from adults and here you play an enormous role in helping them to develop such positive self-concepts. I was seeing an African movie some years back and I could recall this particular scene of a young toddler scribbling with a charcoal on a wooden board. Each time he feels he is satisfied, he would walk up to his mother and show her with excitement in his eyes. The woman in turn claps for him and he goes back again to repeat the same process. It was quite funny because all the child needed was just support and love from the mother. And that's why I recall that the first rule in children art is this: Never call any work or art "not beautiful" or something negative. The child see's the world different from yours. That drawing or painting is perfect. It may happen that when toddlers are not acting so positively from the adult's perspective, they are only trying to assert their ever increasing independence just to gain more control over their world. Autonomy can be very energizing and once a child could have this, the world would become so big for his little mind. He/she begins to grow this do-it yourself mentality. And most of the time they actually need our help but end up making a mess of the whole thing. It would come to a particular point in time when mothers and fathers would begin to wonder how their child learnt the most heated declaration, "No". This comes as a result of the naturally acquired growing sense of selfhood which make toddlers showcase oppositional behavior, with "no" being the functional powerful word. Most of the time, adults tend to overestimate the capabilities of children as they leave infancy and would want from them behaviors that may not be realistic or just too complex for a child to understand. But ironically, the competencies of young infants are usually underestimated

Toddlers are in the stage of solitary play from 18 to 24 months, but from two to three years, they become gradually aware of one another. Although, much interaction could be lacking here, they proceed to the stage of parallel play i.e. the child definitely plays independently, but the activity chosen naturally consciously or unconsciously brings him to the children around him. He/she plays with toys around or beside other kids but still plays alone. But the level of imitation becomes high as he/she would want to copy what another child might be doing. As this continues, compassions comes in, understanding, display of friendship and even other act of kindness like sharing. All these happen by the neurobiology of the child's brain.

The last part of this chapter would be spent on actually describing the physical and motor skills of toddlers. A one year old toddler would be able to display the following skills:

- He/ she triples the birth weight

- He/she grows to a height of 50% over birth length

- The head circumference equal to that of the chest

- One to eight milk teeth

- He/she can be pulled to stand

- He/she can walk with or without help

- He/she can sit down without help

- Banging two blocks together

- Flipping many pages of a book at a time

- Sleep 8-10 hours a night and take at least two naps.

We also have the following falling under the sensory and cognitive development of a year old:

- He or she is intrigued by a fast moving object and follows it.

- They can respond to sounds

- They can reply to his or her name

- Understand little important words

- Can pronounce some monosyllabic words and some bi-syllabic words including papa and some other words

- They can understand simple commands

- They always try to imitate animal sounds

- A year old toddler could connect names with objects as well as understand that object exist even when they can't see them.

- They can point with index finger

- They can wave bye bye

- Attachment to a toy or object could be developed at this stage.

- They always experience separation anxiety and may cling to parents

- Make brief and quick journeys away from parents just to explore their environment only in a familiar setting.

Vocalization and Socialization aspect of a toddler are seen below:

- 15 months old could use 10-15 words

- They could say "NO"

- They could also indicate when diaper is wet.

- A toddler of 18 month could use phrase composed of adjectives and nouns

- They begin to have temper tantrums

- They become ritualistic, like having a favorite toy or blanket

- Thumb sucking could become inevitable if not controlled.

We have been able to establish some peculiar attributes of the toddler as well as understanding them. We would move on to an important subtopic in this chapter.

Two Reasons Why Toddlers Don't Follow Their Parent's Direction

Several reasons could exist why children in general don't follow their parent's direction. Most of the time it can be due to disconnection, being over-direct or our child has better things to do. But whatever reason it may be, your child has a right not to listen to you. They can make their own decision just as you can make yours. You may feel a little bit uncomfortable with what I just said, but that's just how it is. That aside. Below, I would give some experiences to open your minds to this topic. Names have been changed for some reasons.

"My daughter is 2.5 years old and when we go to activities (structured playgroups, mom toddler stuff) she does not follow direction (or very rarely will follow direction). Maybe she will to a degree, but generally speaking she is the wild flower that is rolling around, running and dancing circles in the big open room while all the other kids are sitting quietly by their moms' side. . . should I be concerned about this? Or leave her to her own exploration (it's winter here so the big open space to run is really treat!) or keep on trying to get her to listen to the 'animator' who is trying to run a session?"

Definitely, in the above, the child has something better to do. I would run through some reasons toddlers do the otherwise of what they are told and would provide some practical solutions.

The first reason a toddler wouldn't do as you say as a parent may be that both of you are disconnected. Disconnection could cause more than we can imagine. And this can happen for a variety of reasons. Sometimes, we might have made the common mistake of taking our child's age appropriate resistant behavior personally. Most times, children tend to repeat their resistant and rebellious behaviors because our love can't be felt. They feel that they are out of favor with us, misunderstood and blamed when what they need at the present is our help. Sometimes, our behavioral control tactics which may be usually applied with more than enough dose of anger can make the child uncomfortable. Secondly, sometimes, words are not enough. A flash of a video I saw online some years ago, just found its way to my mind now. I recalled a little child of 16-19 months hitting his father repeatedly, even after the father cautioned him. When this happen, we are always taken aback. We start thinking, has this baby suddenly become evil, has he stopped loving us? No, he/she maybe having a hard time trying to verbalize something very crucial for a demonstration. For example, you have your child up in your arms and he hits you. You hold her flailing hands while you reassure her, "I won't let you hit me. That hurts." If she continues with the other hand, you can add "you are having a hard time not hitting, so I will put you down." Then what happens, she bursts into tears. Now take a look from this angle, you have taken the action necessary to prevent her from further upsetting you.

Another reason may be that we are over-directing. Toddlers aren't robots, you don't order them around. You should provide them with choices, autonomy, and free-will sometimes. And that is why I said earlier "your child has a right not to listen to you." Let's face the fact here, children love to be active participants in life beginning at birth. They love to be the central of attraction and they love to be an adult, even though they are not. Always include toddlers in decisions and ask them to help you. Together you can both make a good team.

Roni Leiderman, associate dean of the Family Center at Nova Southeastern University in Forth Lauderdale, Florida says this:

"Toddlers are just like the rest of us-they don't always listen. At their age, they need you to teach them how to pay attention, but what often happens is that parents say something 10 times, then they start counting down to punishment. That doesn't teach a child to listen, but to ignore 10 times before paying attention when you are about to lose it"

Making them listen to you can be very hard but it get simple once you have mastered some few tricks which we would discuss later on, but for now here are some:

- When talking to them, you come down to their level. This would help you to have a good eye contact and it works best when you are face to face with your child.

- Let your message be clear, simple and authoritative. State the instruction clearly; "come climb into your car seat, okay, sweetie" "It is cold outside, I want you to put on your sweater"

- Follow through with the instruction(s) you are giving, don' t make threats or promises you won ' t keep.

- Be sure your partner shares your rules, respects them and upholds them

- Reinforce your message with actions. Like when your child is in absorbing activity, like a video game. The usual "Time for bed!" wouldn' t do, you put off the Monitor or T.V as the case may be.

- Give warnings. When I say warnings, I mean simple, detailed instruction beforehand. Like before leaving the house you can say, "We' re going to leave in a few minutes. When I call you, you stop playing with your toys and get ready."

- Notice the good doings of your child and appreciate them. Catch your child being good. Like, "Put your toys away⋯ Good job!"

- As a parent, you should have a good behavior. To serve as a model to your children.

Five Toddler Personality Types

Toddler personality differs according to personal study. Some experts say we have three personality types, while others say we have four. Some even extend the list to five. But the most important thing here is to know that just as we as adults have personality types, toddlers are not exempted. They don't act the same way, they have their peculiarities. Toddlers display a confusing array of personality traits. Some can be mischievous, boisterous etc. Quickly, I would run through five toddler personality types:

Shy Charlotte/Sean

These are toddlers who take refuge behind you whenever visitors arrive. They are clingy and they need you to be there for them. You should not use the phrase s/he's shy to people when explaining your child behavior. More also, allow them to cling to you if that is what they want. As a parent, you should build the confidence of your child. And how can you do this? Be proud of them anytime anywhere. Tell him how beautiful the drawing he made is.

Confident Chloe/Clive

They are amazing and very bright. Nothing stops them from interacting with others. They make friends with any child they see and could talk to strangers. They are flamboyant and they don't hide their feelings. As a parent, you should promote friendliness, generosity, kindness and all other good traits in your child at their tender age and when they are getting older. Since they have so much confidence running through their veins, they tend to talk a lot. Discourage them from divulging secrets to strangers, if they know any.

High-Spirited, Sam

Is he easily distracted? Can you calm him down by just offering him something different, something not to familiar? Do they get so bored easily? Do they find it hard to concentrate for so long? Well your child falls under this category. Or do you have a child who sprinkles cereal on the sofa, empties the cupboard of anything he can think of, they derive fun in it. Well you really need to put people like this close. They should not be far from. A child who falls under this personality type should learn how to tidy up the mess he made, you can turn it into a game if you have to. Protect your products in the home.

Hot tempered Harry

They are the fathers and mother of all tantrums. They kick their legs, turn bright red, and scream all over the place. Every toddler could be a mother or father of tantrums but theirs just happen more frequently. We have discussed extensively on how you could curb this. You can refer back to the above if you still want more clarification. Am sorry to say this, but the bitter truth is that parents of children who fall under this category have hell of a work to do and may end up exhausted at the end of the day.

Easy-going Eli/Ella

They are calm, collected and they play nicely with other kids. They don't cause any anxiety. Parents love children who display this traits. You can take advantage of their laid-back personality by empowering them with words of knowledge from books and chatting with them to improve literary skills. They enjoy feeling lonely and it takes a lot to pull them out of their shell, even though they are little kids. Surround them with playmates with different temperaments and notice how they act.

Chapter 2

Communicating With Toddlers

Eleven Principles of Effective Communication For Good Relationship

Communication serves as the basis for any kind of relationship, be it a marriage relationship, mother- father relationship, parent to child, child to another child etc. The roles of communication in any relationship cannot be overemphasized. Now, we are talking about toddlers her and even the roles of communication applies to them the most.

First, what is communication? The very definition of communication is the exchange of ideas from each side with adequate feedback. When the possibility of exchange of ideas is blocked, then the likelihood of reaching a mutual understanding is reduced. Effective communication includes sending the message you want to deliver, in a way it can be understood by the other party and receiving an immediate response. Communication is very important in families as it allow each member respect the wants and needs of each other. We definitely love our children and what them to grow up happy, healthy and responsible, then we really need to work on our communication skills. Why is effective communication important? It is, because our children also love us and want our guidance, support and approval. An effective communication modifies the way your child would communicate with others, from communication children learn values from our words, our postures and our tones. An effective communication skill with our children helps us to address problems or situations in a positive and healthy way. Having established this fact that communication serve as the base for a good relationship we need to know if good relationship or effective communication is really possible. Yes and yes, it is possible, below are some basic principles of good parent/child communication:

1. You can communicate without the interest of the other party. You need to let your child know that you are interested in him or her, you are involved and you are ready to help when needed.

2. Give your child all attention when he is communicating. Turn off the television, put the newspaper down, and raise your gaze from your mobile phone.

3. Make sure your conversations are private except if any other person is involved.

4. Embarrassment would only cause resentment and hostility. Don't embarrass them. You may be surprised that this applies to toddlers too.

5. You should get down to your child's level when you want to talk, don't tower over your child.

6. If you are angry, regain your temper before making an attempt to communicate.

7. Be an active listener and try to make an effort to be one even when you are tired. Genuine active listening is very difficult and hard work. We would talk more about this in this chapter.

8. Don't jump into conclusions when your children are opening up to you. Even if toddlers sometimes communicate incoherently most of the time, they are still saying something, they still want to tell you something. Be patient to listen to them.

9. Assist him or her to take the right steps when they come for advice.

10. Encourage the child's attempt to communicate, praise his or her effort. Children need a lot of encouragement and support at their tender age.

11. Don't use foul languages or words which put others down. Toddlers tend to imitate everything

they see and hear. When I say everything, I mean everything.

This chapter would be very empty and incomplete without explaining the importance of words of encouragement and praise. As a parent, you should know that children thrive on positive attention and you are to give that to them. You can make use of some of the following phrases or all:

Yes Good Fine... .

Excellent!

That's right Correct

Wonderful! I like the way you do that...

I'm impressed

I am proud of you

That's good Wow!

Much better

You are really improving at. . .

You showed a lot of responsibility . . .

I appreciate the way you . . .

You are great at . . .

I am sure glad you are my son/daughter. . .

I LOVE YOU

You can also learn to show them how you fell by telling them the following:

Smile for me...

High five

A pat on your shoulder.

Scatter their hair gently with your fingers and smile.

You can tickle them, laugh with them, and give them a warm hug.

"If a child lives with criticism, he learns to condemn. If a child lives with hostility, he learns to fight. If a child lives with ridicule, he learns to be shy. If a child lives with fear, he learns to be shy. If a child lives with fear, he learns to be apprehensive. If a child lives with shame, he learns to feel guilty. If a child lives with encouragement he learns to be confident. If a child lives with acceptance, he learns to love. If a child lives with recognition, he learns it is good to have a goal. If a child lives with fairness, he learns justice. If a child lives with security, he learns to have faith in himself and those about him. If a child lives with friendliness, he learns the world is a nice place in

which to live to love and be loved."

-Anonymous

I wonder why a wonderful quote like the above should be anonymous, well it explains itself, what more can I say?

The other part of this chapter is going to talk more exclusively on listening in communication.

SLLR Method of Becoming An Active Listener

Just as we have explained that the importance of communication cannot be overemphasized in any relationship as well as toddler to parent relationship. It is fundamental for us to know how to listen in communication. It has been established that the mind of a toddler is adventurous, just like any other child. He wants to explore the world, understand more than you are letting him and do more than you can allow. They are always communicating to family, friends and even their toys. Remember we mentioned the imaginative aspect of their memory and how it helps growth, learning and behavioral make up. Their imaginative minds communicate with their toys, they turn a moving car into something quite different from what it is and other things around them. In the vocalization and socialization aspect of a toddler we see that when he/she is `15 months old, the ability to use 10-15 words is harnessed and fully utilized, the ability to say no, the ability to indicate when diaper is wet and also the ability to use phrase composed of adjectives and nouns becomes useful. These are all manners or forms of communication and our duty is to listen.

Picture this:

You are in a child care center, 19 month-old Gift is clinging to you, her and crying as they enter. You pull Gift's hands from your arm, saying, "Don't be such a crybaby and go play." You walk into the pediatrician's waiting room in another instance and Daniel climbs dangerously high on a furniture. He throws his toy at his mother when she calls his name. Instead of doing the needful, his mother laughs nervously and says quietly, "I don't know what to do with him." In another instance one year-old Melissa yanks on a locked kitchen cabinet while her father is cooking. He finds her and says, "Oh-I see you are trying to get into this cabinet, but these glass pans are for me only. Let's make a drawer with some plastic kitchen things for you. You can use them to while I cook."

The above scenarios show us that child-parent interactions is differ from each other. You can see that the interaction between Melissa and her father is harmonious and developmentally appropriate.

Young children including toddlers feel valued when parents listen to what they have to say. We all know that listening to kids is not always easy, but children think differently and sometimes they may not have the words to express themselves plainly. Listening is more than just hearing, it all about understanding the feelings embedded in the child's words and taking the positive action. In listening, for the soul aim of having a good relationship with your child, active listening should be employed.

What is active listening? Active listening is the best type of listening. Even in learning and other types of relationship. Here, it involves giving your child your undivided attention when he/she seeks you out for conversation. It's not just hearing, it requires using your intellect, feelings and even physical response to attract, attain and give information about your interaction. In active listening, you can use the following Stop-Look-Listen-Respond (SLLR) method:

1. **Stop:** You should stop whatever you are doing and pay attention to your child whenever they try communicating. Children love attention, and once you give that to them they open up, they need you to be focused on them.

2. **Look:** This is where we really need to know the importance of eye contact, facial expressions and body language. As a parent, you should look for nonverbal cues which may give you a hint on your child' s thought and feelings.

3. **Listen:** Listen to what he/she is trying to say. Make up for the lapse in incoherent words and pay special attention to the tone of voice. Is he sounding angry? You should realize that they may be communicating in several messages and most may be unspoken.

4. **Respond:** make sure you use eye contact during the conversation and nods, "mmm-hmms" . Smile, touch to confirm your attentiveness and make the necessary adjustment.

Seven Parenting Attributes to Build Great Relationship

Building a good relationship entails a lot, and one of it is making a relationship deposit. Imagine a deposit jar where you have coins labelled as praise, hugs, high fives, play, listen, etc. You have a good relationship with your child if you make these deposits. Even as a parent, it may not be easy to build a firm relationship with your child than building relationship with others. Having said that, you should make these deposits a regular thing in your relationship with your child, each day you should show all or at least some of the relationship building attributes. Here are the seven parenting attributes for building positive relationships with a child:

1. Spend quality time with your child. Both of you can work on a project together.

2. Acknowledge the child's effort in anything. Give encouragement for positive behaviors such as hugs, high fives, thumbs up after accomplishing task.

3. Make use of empathy, a relationship-building strategy that helps you interact and value what you have.

4. Play games with him or her and play outside.

5. Post your child's work on social media, your computer screen or hang them on you walls.

6. Ask them questions every time. With this you get an update on what they like and don't.

7. Make sure you adopt your child's ideas and stories. Especially when painting or participating in any activity, give them that freedom.

As you build positive relationship with your child, your potential influence the child's behavior and grows exponentially. This means that children cue in on the presence of meaningful and caring adults. They attend differentially and selectively and this gives me the impression that what you give is what you get. Listen to what they really want and give that to them. I must confess, communication is not easy, but it is necessary. Strengthening the relationship that exist between you and your child through active listening, influences the future of the child.

Chapter 3

Dealing With Difficult Toddlers

We have established that toddlers can be difficult, and the need to train them comes in. We should not just claim that they would understand when they are grown, no. it may be too hard for you to stop it when they are grown. They are toddlers, they are not dumb, and they know the difference between right and wrong. Remember the introduction, we are getting to the core of this book and I would want you to read this with an open mind. All am saying here, may not go well with your thinking but an open mind would make you think from different angles.

Four Common Struggles Toddlers May Have

To begin, we need to understand why toddlers could be difficult. For the first time, they are realizing that they are separate individuals from their parents and/or caregivers. The initial thought of an infant is that he/she is part of the parent but when they reach the toddler stage they realize that this isn't true. This also means that they become driven to assert themselves to communicate their likes and dislikes as well as trying to act independently. They are also trying to develop the language skills which will help them express their wants, ideas or needs.

Furthermore, toddlers do not understand the logic of waiting and the logic behind having everything. They no nothing or little about self-control and in a nut shell, he/she may be having a hard time balancing his/her needs with what you are providing as a parent or care giver. Toddlers could be difficult, they could be funny to. Here are four common situations your child could be struggling with:

1. He says no when he means yes. These happens when you are offering him a favorite treat.

2. He has a meltdown anytime you fail to understand his words.

3. He doesn't want any substitute. The blue pajamas or nothing else, even though they may not be washed or even after offering him the purple one.

4. He acts out when frustrated. Gives up everything when angry.

What is listed above are only acts which toddlers put on to manage strong feelings, since they are new to almost everything, they lack good control over what controls them and how they can control it. They are toddlers, they soon find out that they have vocal powers and that is when the crying, shouting and yelling increases. They may also want to try to make different noises to see how they sound and the reactions of adults around them to such noise. They impulsively go into an activity without much or any thinking. It is important for you to know that there exist a peculiarity in each child. They react differently to different situations, in fact you can even place a tag around them. Most times you can start with some funny names like bubbly, daredevil, determined, stubborn, cautious, adventurous etc. It may interest you to know that some challenging toddler behavior is developmentally correct, they may be defiant, bossy, sassy or impulsive but they are just byproduct of what the child needs-independence.

Eleven Difficult Behaviors and Their Practical Solutions

Unfortunately, some bad behaviors are common among toddlers. Here are the eleven difficult behaviors and their practical solutions:

1. Aggression, hitting and biting

2. Interrupting

3. Lying

4. Pulling hair

5. Running away

6. Screaming

7. Tattling

8. Teasing

9. Throwing tantrums

10. Throwing things

11. Whining

Aggression, Hitting And Biting

Aggressive behavior is normal for toddlers, don't be surprised I said so. Now, I would provide you with practical solutions on what you are to do when you come across an aggressive toddler.

- Make sure you keep your cool: keeping your cool shows how controlled you are, don't yell at the child when he/she is in the aggressive mode. If you tell your child she is bad, you are just getting her riled up.

- Let's your limits be clear: Your reply to your aggressive toddler should be immediate. Make sure he/she is out of the situation for a brief time-out. Maybe a minute or two should give him/her time to cool down. Thereafter, you connect to the child after he/she has understood the consequences of the reaction.

- Strengthen good behavior: I have mentioned this point behavior and would still say it again. Make sure you reward good behavior immediately you see it. You should not give your child attention only when he is misbehaving, catch him doing something good and praise him for it. An offer to push his swing or play together should be a reward for good behavior.

- Provide logical consequences: If your child begins to throw Lego toys at other children while they are playing, take him or her away immediately and watch others play. During that process, explain that he/she can go back when she is ready to have fun without hurting other children. Don't lecture or try to think like a toddler. You can't reason with them for now because they don't really understand the consequences of their actions.

- Make discipline to be consistent: Children enjoy rote learning and with that, bits of information remain where there are stored. Make sure you respond to each episode of aggression the same way, so much you become predictable. This forms a pattern that the child recognizes and tries to avoid. This will eventually sink into their consciousness.

- Alternatives should be taught: Explain to him or her briefly on the consequences of his or her last action. It is natural to have angry feelings but it is not okay to show them by kicking, hitting, or biting. He should apologize after lashing out someone for any reason. Such an apology should be sincere even though it may look insincere to you. With these, the lesson will sink in.

- Keep your toddler active: If you notice your child is a high spirited one, give her plenty of unstructured time, make them outdoors preferably. This gives him much time to burn off abundance of energy.

- Watch it: When it comes to screen time, as a parent you should watch whatever your child is watching. Not all cartoons are meant for children. Be mindful of the digital games and other media designed for young children. Several studies suggest that extreme screen time contributes to the bad behavior of a child and causes much problem as they grow. It may interest you to know that The American Academy of Pediatrics advises against TV and other screen which includes phones, computers and tablets until children are at least 18 months old. Even if your child is 18 months old, you should limit his screen time to not more than an hour a day. Choose what she is watching, and choose high-quality, age-appropriate media. A war movie with a lot of battle scenes wouldn't be good for an aggressive child. It would only upgrade his level of aggressiveness into something bloody or extreme.

- Get help if you need help: Speak to a child doctor if you notice that your child's aggression is too much. But this should be when you have noticed some or all of the following features:

  ✓ Your child finds it easy to attack adults.

✓ He or she enjoys making other children upset or frightened

✓ He or she remains aggressive for more than a few weeks after you have tried all you could.

Interrupting

Nothing can be so exasperating than a child who obviously break in every time you are chatting with a friend. Toddlers don't really interrupt with words all the time but their actions. And that is because they always seek attention from their parents and may be jealous if a friend or an adult is getting all of it. In this aspect, it is your fault. You can do the following:

- Chose the right locale for your meetings. A place where your child can play while you talk with the adult. A park having a sandbox is something nice.

- Get a baby sitter. This would help a lot and would allow you use all focus or concentration during the meeting. Knowing that your child is in safe hands.

- Teach your children polite behavior. A good way to teach them is by reading them some books like The Berenstain Bears Forget Their Manners, by Stan and Jan Berenstain or The Bad Good Manners Book, by Babette Cole's Aliki's Manners and What Do you Say, Dear? By Sesyle Joslin. Any book on good manners you can lay your hands on. Read it to them every day.

- Schedule your phone calls. You wouldn't want your child to disturb you while you are on a call, so make necessary preparations.

Lying

First, why do children lie? They have active imagination and they are very forgetful. These cute angels may also have what we call angel syndrome. A child who thinks that his parents believe he can do know wrong would do wrong on purpose. When asked, a lie comes to mind. Toddlers do lie, and it is natural for them to do so. How can you stop this?

- Always encourage truth-telling. You should not be mad at your child when he or she tells you the truth instead you should be happy. Show your child that honesty pays off.

- You should not accuse your child for any reason. Your comments, remarks should help your child not put him down.

- Don't weigh your child down with too many expectations. He or she would not understand. They are children, toddlers not adults. You shouldn't be expecting too much from them.

- Build your trust. Assure your child that you trust him or her and don't puncture that trust.

Pulling Hair

To begin with, pulling hair, biting, pinching, hitting etc. are ways your child showcases his feelings or applies control over what seems to be his immediate environment (his body). Roberts, a professor of clinical psychology at Idaho State University in Pocatello claims that "a child might be pulling hair to make bad things go away." For whatever reason, you should take the following steps when these happens:

- Let him or her know that it doesn't work. Demonstrating convincingly that an aggressive action would get your child nowhere is a key to suppressing aggression. Don't ignore it, demonstrate the futility of pulling hair and make sure he understands it.

- Stop the behavior as soon as it starts. When you catch him holding a fistful of hair, stop him immediately. Hold his hand firmly while you keep repeating this sentence "we don't pull hair. Pulling hair hurts."

- Take your time to give a detailed explanation, but make sure it is very brief. You start by asking him or her "what did you do that was wrong?" after the reply, you make use of that opportunity to tell him that pulling his hair only hurts himself and others.

- You should not be guilty of the same offense. Don't pull your child's hair if you don't want them to pull it also.

Running Away

A running away toddler could be very funny. Like really? Where do they think they are going? But you have to be careful when this happens outdoors, especially on the walkway. Why do they run? Just like any other attitude displayed by a toddler, running away comes from a new sense of independence and the fact that he has legs that can run. Patricia Shimm, director of the Barnard College Center for Toddler Development in New York and co-author of Parenting Your Toddler says "toddlers love the feeling of being free and running around, you can encourage it as long as you can control where they run." You can't stop this, you can only control it:

- Stay close to them and it should be okay for you to look ahead, when they are running.

- Show him where he can run and where he can't. Allow him to explore the safe areas

- Entertain your child.

Screaming

There are many reasons why toddlers scream. Most of the time, toddlers scream to get attention or demand for something. And we all know that a toddler's scream is very annoying. Screaming can be very embarrassing and when the toddler's volume is turned way up, it only aggravates you. You can do the following to curb this act:

- You might want to run errands on your child schedule. Isn't the he dictating what he wants here? Oh yes he is and he has a right to do so. To save your eardrums, do the right thing at the right time.

- You might want to stick to noisy restaurants when out. This only covers your secret and it becomes less embarrassing.

- Encourage your child to make use of indoor voice. A simple shuu... while you place your finger on your lips is enough gesticulation for him or her to understand you.

- Make shouting a game. This may sound ridiculous but once in a while, play a shouting game with your child. Indulge his need to be loud by saying, "Let's both yell as loud as we can," join him and after some seconds, make him stop by saying "Now, let's see who can whisper best"

- Keep your child occupied.

- Don't yell at your child. They imitate you, and it wouldn't take long for them to catch the screaming feeling.

Tattling

Why do children tattle? According to Jerry Wyckoff, a child psychologist in Prairie village, Kansas. "Tattling allow a child to one-up another child, to gain favor in the eyes of her parent or teacher." Some of the time, kids tattle because they have not developed the social or emotional skills required to solve skills all by themselves. Tattling has a positive effect too and it means that your child is showing you that he/she understands the rules and knows right from wrong. Before we go too far, what is tattling? It just simply means telling somebody, especially somebody in authority about something bad or the wrong doing of somebody else. Do you get report from your child about everything? "Mom, Michael is playing in that person's car, Dad, Sarah is keeping a crayon in her pocket, Mom, Brian is playing with a sharp object . . . etc." That's tattling. The following steps can be taken:

- Assess the situation: "it is hard for kids this age (toddler age) to make independent judgments about what's tattle-worthy and what isn't" Wyckoff said. Before you conclude that your child is a whiny tattletale, take a stock of the situation.

44

- Put the work back on his shoulder for tattling. When your child understands that tattling only gets him more responsibility, he tends to mind his own business.

Teasing

You may agree or not, teasing is just what life brings. It happens when it happens and even toddlers are not left out of it. It is really painful when toddlers are teased and you should understand that as a parents. What can you do when a toddler is teased? This may not work well for toddlers as they would require verbal response.

- Your child should not respond. This could be hard but it is a trick which can repel those guilty of the teasing offense.

- You can coach your child to "agree" with what the teaser is saying. He/she would look dumb when a child says "I agree I suck my thumb"

- Ask for help. Your child can ask for help from anyone or any adult around.

Throwing Tantrums

Of all the bad behaviors toddlers display, throwing tantrums seems to be the worse of them all. A temper tantrum can be equivalent to a summer storm. Something fierce and sudden. One minute, you and your child are in the middle of a perfect dinner, another he is whining and whimpering. As if that is not enough, she begins to scream at the top of her lungs. Kids of ages 1 to 3 are prone to this. Quickly, I would provide seven tips on how to handle a tantrum:

- First rule is that you don't lose your cool. There is nothing pretty about tantrum. In fact a child may add kicking, screaming pounding on the floor, holding his breath to the point of turning blue, etc. I know, this is very hard to handle, but he rest assured that when a child is having a tantrum, he or she is just trying to withhold his actual behavior. Don't lose yourself by getting overly frustrated. It may interest you to know that some experts suggest that you should calmly leave the room for a few minutes and return after your child has stopped crying but in this process, you should keep watch of the child. While some may recommend that you pick the child and hold him or embrace her some may disagree that what you have just done is just to encourage the child. You may want to employ the traditional try and error thing. Keep your calm and see what works best for your child.

- Always remember that you are an adult not a kid. I noticed a child in a child care once. When he was having his tantrums, the child care giver was presenting him with a lot of things, he kept throwing them at her. No matter how long a tantrum might continue, you should not provide anything for the child. Tantrums should not be the good way for him to express his feeling.

- Make use of a time-out occasionally. This depends on the age of the child. A time out could help him or her realize what must have gone wrong. Explain briefly, and give out punishment. I know you may be surprised when I say punishment, yes! Punishment. They need to be punished for misbehaving. Here comes another question, how do I punish a child of 18 months?

- Once you have noticed any situation that may be prone to tantrums, you stay away from it. If you notice that he falls apart when he is hungry, a snack pack with you is no crime. If trouble exist when he or she wants to make transition from one activity to the next, you should be ready to give heads-up before the change occurs. Toddlers love to get the independent feeling, so they always prefer one thing from the other. They love to make choices, monitor how often you say no to their choices and how often they also say no to yours.

- Show love to your child. Letting your child know that you love him after any tantrum could have two contrasting causes. One, a quick hug and telling him that you love him could silence him or otherwise. As a parent, you should show love to your child every time. Make them feel proud to have you as a parent not only when tantrums happen.

- Even though daily tantrums are perfect normal part of the mid-toddler years, keeping an eye out for possible problems is very important. When having an extremely busy schedule could cause parental tension. All these can provoke tantrums.

Throwing Things

Throwing things is an enjoyable skill for many children between 18 months to 3 years. Naturally they just love throwing things and has nature would have it, it just take some fine simple, motor skills to open the fingers and let go of an object to any possible direction. Throwing things is fun for the toddlers. You are always mad when spaghetti winds up all over your just mopped kitchen floor but for a toddler, it is great fun and a perfect experience. What can you do about it? You really can't do anything about you just have to control it:

- Show him what can be thrown. If she is encouraged to throw, she would   learn what not to throw. When you provide a lot of thing to throw like balls, etc. she would understand that there are somethings which can be throne and some other things which are meant to be kept. Playing throwing games can be very beneficial too.

- Don't encourage aggressive throwing. Pull him out from playing when he shows signs of aggressive throwing which may hurt anyone. The key is to be brief, smart and disciplined. Whenever he gets angry.

- Make clean up fun. Clean up with your child. Tell him to pick up everything he must have thrown. It may been an overwhelming task for a child's age, yes! But you wouldn't allow him to do much. Just make him know that throwing things is no good.

- Make sure you use toddler-proof dishes. You should not make use of fine china or even breakable stoncwarc. This is safety and you should understand this.

Whining

Whining is natural to toddlers because they rely on adult for almost everything. How can a child get your attention so as to obtain what he needs? Whining of course. A child whines when he feels powerless and he has a pressing need. What can you do to stop it?

- Define what you mean by whining. Some experts suggest that you can record your child, both in mid-whine and during normal conversation and when both of you are good, you can play it back and discuss about it. Point out whining, let him understand what it means.

- Understand that your child needs attention and give it to her. Whenever your child request for something in a pleasant way, make sure you respond immediately. Even if you cannot answer his request, acknowledge the request and give him a short estimate of time. Be realistic, don't promise what you can't achieve.

Chapter 4

Disciplining Toddlers

Most times, parents don't want to enforce rules, they don't want to discipline children because they don't want to be the villain. They don't want to trouble their kids. Well, what I would say is this. "Give them enough trouble, lest they would trouble you in the future" there are some few aspects you should know about discipline.

First, we need to make a distinct line between discipline and punishment. Jo Frost, in her Supernanny show presents discipline as well as punishment in her bid to manage the child's behavior. Discipline is a way to teach the child self-control while punishment is what a child receives when there is no self-control. As simple as that.

Why do toddlers need rules? Like everyone in the world, when there is no rule, there is no sin. Everything goes, a complete state of anarchy. Rules also serve as boundaries set for your child to make them think and act orderly. Since discipline is not the same as punishment, then we should keep it positive. Physical aggression is not okay, aim at teaching the child how to behave. As much as I would love to say this, I would also want you to understand me. This book isn't a holy grail or a map for toddler care. It is a guide, sieve what you think is useless. Discipline your child when you really don't want to. There shouldn't be any lapse. Although, you may feel that this is strict. I consider it not to be. Let your rules be your rules and don't make them hard.

Discipline vs Punishment

We have discussed little about this in the introductory paragraphs of this chapter, but that doesn't stop us from doing justice to the subtopic.

A 1985 study shows a correlation between what seems to be corporal punishment, stealing, truancy, aggression, hostility, and depression, lying and low self-esteem etc. Now what is the role of punishment? Punishment, when focused on the wrong direction causes children to put all their attention on anger toward an "unfair" adult instead of learning responsible actions-the sole aim of punishment. In fact, punishment when channeled in the wrong way validates fear, intimidation, pain and even violence. Punishment can turn a parent into an executioner and can even escalate into battering. Battering could lead to mental, spiritual and emotional harm. In contrast to discipline which provides an avenue for dialogue and communication and teaches the child how to control himself in a social order. According to Michigan State University Extension, punishment and discipline are very different and have separate outcomes for children and distinct impacts on parents as well as caregivers. Discipline is not spanking or telling your child she is missing dinner, that's punishment. Now when a child is punished negatively, the information you giving him is this. "Don't let me ever see you doing that again! Or I better not catch you doing that again" which means the child can continue his bad actions but must not be caught. Then the child learns to be careful. This has never been and would never be a good way of managing behavior.

The word discipline is derived from the word disciple which means to teach. In this context of child relationship and responsibility, self-control is key. We believe that over time, children would take ownership of inappropriate actions and understand their consequence but can we wait till then? Punishment could come in the form of spanking, insulting, blaming or even humiliating. Barbara Coloroso eloquently describes three different types of parenting in her book entitled Kids are worth it! Giving your child the Gift of Inner Discipline (1995) She suggests that parents can either adhere to brick wall (strict), backbone (consistent in disciplining techniques) and jellyfish (relentless and inconsistent) style of parenting. Parents try to develop any style on their own which falls between these ones to foster and instill respect, warmth and good communication.

Fifteen Habits to Nurture Long-Term Child Discipline

Positive parenting requires positive discipline and this means your child should develop positive values as well as social skills. Please note that positive parenting should not be confused with letting your child do whatever he or she wants. Positive parenting involves parenting in a warm, kind and a very respectful way. Your boundaries should be firm and relevant. Consequences of each action should be reasonable enough. Providing a loving environment should be your goal as a parent. The more positive attention and encouragement you give your child, the more they will respond to you. Positive parenting also requires you to use a polite and respectful tone when communicating with your child. Here are the seven fundamental principles of positive discipline:

1. Tell children what they can do instead of what they cannot do.
2. Protect and preserve children's feelings that they are lovable and capable.
3. Offer children choices only when you are willing to abide by their decisions.
4. Change the environment instead of the child's behavior.
5. Work with children instead of against them.

6. Give children safe limits that they can understand. Recognizing their feelings without accepting their actions. Maintain your authority calmly and consistently. When children break the rules allow them to experience the consequences of their behavior.

7. Set a good example. Speak and act only in ways you want children to speak and act.

8. Avoid power struggles. Explain why a rule is set or why others are enforced/established. It is important to communicate and provide adequate details about the rule. Children are grateful for explanations instead of just saying "no".

9. Take timeouts when necessary. Timeouts are simply a break and chance or opportunity for you and your child to start over fresh. According to Kathy Lynn, author of Who's in Charge Anyway, "timeout is not a place, it's a state of mind."

10. Avoid being patronizing, insulting or verbally inappropriate (i.e yelling, blaming). This form of parenting will in turn decrease the child's self-esteem. Comparison to other children and favoritism also could negatively impact the child's disposition.

11. Enforce realistic expectation, consequences and consistent communication of behavior. Define fair, firm and consistent follow-through.

12. Model positive behavior (i.e. actions, behavior and communication).

13. React at a normal voice level, not out of anger, tiredness or other negative emotions.

14. Discuss clarity in rules and behaviors, verbally and non-verbally.

15. Involve children in some family rule making. The child, in turn will feel empowered and more confident.

You should know in the long run that effective discipline evolves over time. Such discipline should be very consistent as well as age appropriate. Sometimes, you could bring two contrasting ideas when you try to explain inappropriate behavior and still want the child the express how they are feeling. Their feelings may just be inappropriate and they don't know. Here, you need to have a good understanding of the reason or the motive behind every action. When you are resolving the true underlying issues and when making further preclude future problems and negative repercussions, you need this understanding.

Appropriate Discipline for Different ages

Below are appropriate discipline for different ages.

0-1 year old

A waste of time to discipline them, like some people say. But loving touch and gentle words. Whatever the baby does may not be to get at you. It is not to be naughty.

1-3 years

Children are full of curiosity and life. They learn by touching and trying things out. And most of the time they make a mess of using things. Toddlers enjoy doing things on their own and get frustrated when they don't have the skills. The following are appropriate discipline methods:

- Keep instructions simple and make sure you take one lesson and a time.

- Avoid battles. This happens when a child is having a tantrum. Don't struggle with him or her. Simple words like "You've had enough. . . Okay, let's get you down from your high chair" could go a long way.

- You may want to distract them by engaging them in any activity of your choice, because most times they don't know the consequences of their behavior and how to change it.

3-4 years (Preschoolers)

Here, children fully understand most of the instructions given to them. They are really excited and they could be very hard to control. The following process can be taken when it comes to discipline:

- Teach the child choices by showing him what is really meant by choices.

- Make sure you think ahead and let your child understand what is coming. The seven steps of discipline as mentioned above must be followed.

5-12 years (Primary school)

At this age, the child fully understands all about himself. He knows his limits and rules, they see things from their own perspective. And as a parent, you need to explain the core of adult behaviors and feelings which may vary. As parents, you should know the following:

- Make sure you discuss with your children a wide range of topics. And it is important you listen to their views. Don't force your ideas on them, because they are entitled to their own feelings.

- Contact other parents, a tree cannot make a forest. Learn how they relate with their children. They may not serve as an example for you because we are not learning formula's which work anywhere in the world.

They are beings and it could happen that they become unpredictable.

- Inculcate the habit of solving problems in your child. Teach him to solve problems in good ways. This is a very useful skill and at this age, it is important for him to be a step towards learning self-discipline.

Chapter 5

Avoiding Six Parenting Mistakes

As parents, we are humans, there is every tendency that we would make mistakes. In fact, this book is full with a lot of mistakes right now. But there are still some common mistakes parents make. We should try as much as we could to avoid such mistakes. Here are six parenting mistakes to avoid:

Being Inconsistent

When it comes to toddlers parenting, do your best to continue in what you might have started. Don't relent. Show your child the consequences of his actions whenever he does wrong. Don't be too tired to do the right thing. The more consistent you are, the more predictable things become, and children learn through rote learning. When it keeps repeating itself, it sticks.

Overdoing Family Time

Spending time with the whole family is fun, but some parents just go to the extreme. Maybe because of over zealousness and happiness. Clinical psychologist Thomas Phelan, author of 1-2-3 Magic says, "Kids cherish time alone with one parent." He point out, "One-one-one time is fun for parent too, because there is no sibling rivalry to contend with."

Offering too much help

Sometimes, children need to figure out things by themselves. Some parents jump into helping them whenever they are faced with trouble. No! Leave them, let them enjoy their liberty. Besty Brown Braun, author of you're Not the Boss of Me, says. "parents who offer too much help may be sabotaging their young children's ability to become self-reliant,"

Talking too much

Phelan, a pediatric psychologist says "Talking can lead to what I call the talk-persuade-argue-yell-hit pattern" as a parent, you don't talk too much. You give short explanations. Don't explain everything, sometimes leave them in the dark, they would figure it out.

Serving only Kiddie Food

Braun says "Children love the fight over food. If we make a fuss about it, it becomes a much bigger deal than it needs to be." Braun's point of view is that, as long as there is something to eat, you don't need to worry. Well, variety, they say is the spice of life. Make sure your toddler is fed with a steady diet of nutritionally irresistible food.

Getting Rid of the Crib

Altmann, a child psychologist says, "Some moms wear themselves out because they have to lie down with their child every night, they don't realize they're the ones who set the pattern." What do cribs do? They promote good sleep habits for the child and the child alone, not you. When a child reaches a height of 35 inches, you should allow him climb out of his crib. It is fun.

Chapter 6

Knowing When And How To Find Help

Just as I have established before now, no man is an island of knowledge. A tree cannot make a forest. You can seek for help everywhere, anywhere. From a child psychologist, from a family friend, anybody.

When seeking help, don't give your child names, don't have a preconceived mind on the kind of child you have, his temperament, his attitudes. Seek help, the right way. When do you need to seek for professional help?

- When your child is vulnerable because of stress and other events of losses he or she must have experienced

- When a child's parent is victim of violence

- When a child's parent has been gone for years. He or she needs advice on how to come back to the life of the child.

Where can you seek professional help?

- Domestic Violence programs

- Health Care providers

- Schools

- Courts

- Mental health providers

- Religious institutions

- Police departments

- District attorneys

CPSIA information can be obtained
at www.ICGtesting.com
Printed in the USA
LVOW10s1922200318

570510LV00012B/1000/P

9 781977 941053